DAYS OF GRACE

Doris Kareva

DAYS OF GRACE

Translated from the Estonian by
MIRIAM McILFATRICK-KSENOFONTOV

BLOODAXE BOOKS

ISBN: 978 1 78037 159 7

First published 2018 by
Bloodaxe Books Ltd,
Eastburn,
South Park,
Hexham,
Northumberland NE46 1BS.

www.bloodaxebooks.com
For further information about Bloodaxe titles
please visit our website or write to
the above address for a catalogue.

ARTS COUNCIL
ENGLAND

EESTI KULTUURKAPITAL

Cover design: Neil Astley & Pamela Robertson-Pearce.

Digital reprint by Lightning Source.

ACKNOWLEDGEMENTS

The poems in this edition have been selected from the following books: *Päevapildid* (Photographs), Eesti Raamat, 1978; *Ööpildid* (Night Shots), Eesti Raamat, 1980; *Puudutus* (Touch), Eesti Raamat, 1981; *Salateadvus* (Secret Consciousness), Eesti Raamat, 1983; *Vari ja viiv* (Shadow and While), Eesti Raamat, 1986; *Armuaeg* (Days of Grace), Eesti Raamat, 1990; *Maailma asemel* (In Place of the World), Loomingu Raamatukogu, 1993; *Hingring* (Soulcircle) Huma, 1996; *Mandragora*, Huma, 2003; *Aja kuju* (Shape of Time), Verb, 2005; *Tähendused* (Meanings), Verb, 2007; *Deka*, Verb, 2008; *Olematuse aiad* (Gardens of Nothingness), Verb, 2012; *Lõpmatuse lävel* (Brink of Infinity), HeadRead, 2015; and also the literary journal *Looming* (Creation), issues 11/2013, 8/2014 and 12/2015.

Some of the translations were previously published in *Windship with Oars of Light* (Huma, 2001), *Pratilipi* (2012), *Lõpmatuse Lävel* (HeadRead, 2015), *Contemporary Estonian Poetry, A Baltic Anthology: Book 3* (University of New Orleans Press, 2013), and in *Indian Quarterly* (2017) where the foreword appeared as a translator's note.

CONTENTS

FOREWORD

Perhaps the clearest expression of what drives Doris Kareva's poetry appears in an article she has written about her father, the composer Hillar Kareva, where she says of both human existence and the act of creation: our means are limited, our possibilities limitless. The article is entitled 'Lesson in Harmony' (*see pages 119-20*) and therein lies the key to Kareva's poetics – a striving for concord between that which seeks expression through language and language which does not allow it to be expressed. At times, a truth seems to be half-hidden / half-revealed in and by the words; at others, the whole momentum of a poem seems to depend solely on the physicality of the words. Words often hint at or flit around an idea or an insight, illuminating in a manner that has been described as oracle-like or like a snowflake on the cusp of disappearance. Most of her poems occupy little space on the page, yet aspire to grasp and articulate something essential in a way that both embodies and defies definition. Sound, meaning and silence overlap and interact to the extent that whole poems appear diamond-like: resilient, incisive and multi-faceted all at once.

The sustained depth and clarity of Kareva's poetry lies in her ability to create ambiguity and suggest harmony at the same time. Over 40 years of poetic output, she has explored the ecstasy and the pain of existence in terms of the sensual and the intellectual. Her poetry evokes and erases the line between the human soul and the universe, between man and god, between voice and silence.

I first encountered Kareva's poetry as a student of the Estonian language when I was given a copy of *Armuaeg* ('Days of Grace') for pronunciation practice. I clearly remember the pleasure I felt in reading her poems aloud; I understood little more than isolated words and phrases, fragments of meaning, but the sounds and rhythm had already captivated me. To translate such poems into English has been to tread a path of discovery of the limits and the potential of my own language.

MIRIAM McILFATRICK-KSENOFONTOV

Pass of Silence

THE CALLING

Yes.
In the beginning was the Word.

I heard and I woke.
Still dazed with dreams
in the dimness I discerned
on the edge of my bed
                    an angel.

He gazed at me in silence –
I was not certain why.

That gaze held sway.

I felt a new and tranquil spirit
take hold of my troubled self.

I had an inkling of aeons,
of what awaits the world –
no sense of unease,
just insight, serene and willing –
            the wisdom of love.

Then he kissed me on the eyes.

I felt the briefest brush of lips
and bliss – a heavenly gift! –
as yet unaware for how grave
                a voyage
I had been blessed.

§

Every day
every night
someone appears,
eyes seared.

Never a word
of what he saw
in the land
of the living.

§

If you speak only once,
the onus is so great
that not a word seems worth
                    saying.

If you live only once,
the prospect is so great
                that you freeze
and speechless let it pass.

§

If I do not speak of this,
I will die.

If I reveal it,
it will kill me.

What – on earth – do I do?

§

Don't call. Don't ask.

My eyes are stalactites
in the cavern of the night.

My heart thuds: a stone axe
in the pain-sparking darkness.

My skull conceals
an oscillograph.

§

In a nightlit room the air blooms.
Half-voiced, eyes closed
they converse – two angels –
over a glinting sword.

Mirror discourse,
steady sporadic silence,
hellbent
ontogenesis.

§

A paw extends in the dark
to probe the flow.
There's no
knowing what will cling to longing.

Raw rough-edged words, terse
and true, translation-proof, from table
to rafters.

Lie there, wordless,
swallow the blood-spit of the dark.

§

My hair grows up through the ceiling
and grapples with clouds that pass

And what becomes of it
I cannot see
and I do not dare to ask

For up there is light
and faces luminous pale
gliding along so sleek

and down here are
beetles, grubs and snails
and clay against my cheek

§

I call you and I sense that you call me.
But I cannot hear if it is so at all.
There are chasms over which no bird
will fly. And silence like a wall.

There are phantasms that petrify the soul.

§

No, this light will not fade
                    from memory.
Just the thought of that March is fraught.

How achingly the sky lightened at dawn!
How alert the teeming tides of thought!

If only one could lie less to oneself.
If only.

What a force that would be.

§

Through life flies a stone of death,
that startles water to a circle.
More and more deeply and distinctly
I have seen you.

You – more me than I am myself.
Human, luminous kindred spirit.
Passing through the dazzle of death
I have felt you.

§

Life has no story,
life is unfolding.

Is it true that we get
all that we wish?

Is it true that we get
all as we deserve?

Is it true that we are caught
by all we evaded?

Time, you fleeting
and far-fetching thing –

life is no story
but hope and honing.

§

When I write,
I shepherd unheeding words
on the nigh impossible slope
of the pass of silence.

When I write,
I practise mastery of shadows
with cool wrist and rapier
on the verge of final darkness.

When I write,
I write an utterly forbidding language;
my ultimate feast is to fast,
the very unearthing of heaven.

§

The future is going on now
right here –
in me and in us.

The idea in your head is a seed.
You are the bud.

And mañana is demain,
man
imbued with nuclear music.

§

Something exploded: was it a bomb
or a poem?

The world shifted –
nothing seems the same.

Static has turned
ecstatic.

In similar vein
believe in blood.

This is your best
expert.

§

To breathe out
you must breathe in.
And vice versa.

Peace is in piecemeal
order in chaos.

All in the grasp of one
whose face is unseen,
whose name is unsaid.

All of us know of him
though not who he is –
love? creation? God?

§

The world is the answer,
man is the question –
still.

Strange persistence.

Bird holds egg,
egg holds needle,
needle holds truth.

Truth has two ends –
one is the point,
the other the eye.

The only plural
is the Maker's world.

§

God occurs.

On a butterfly wing
hieroglyph for the world.

§

What is man?
An angel's shade?
Or a longing cry for concord of souls?

Each of us is an instrument
of God's will and wind:
cherish
and you will be cherished.

§

Pure goodness burns like acid,
a cauterising touch.
The soul stays tender – no end to enduring.
Once felt, forever
fostered.

Day's length does not afford
evening's reward.

Who has given all –
what can he possibly
lack?

Words come back.

§

You shall not
kill.

You shall not kill
your own desire, a distorted grin
on the mouth of murdered requests,
when envy covertly chokes
your amazing grace.

You shall not kill
out of desire, nei-ei-eigh!
on the spirited wishlist horse
that shies, snorts and stamps
to smithereens others'
frailest flowers.

You shall not kill,
but kindle.

Cry all you can –
you shall not kill
your yearning.

§

Middle-aged and overweight
depressive alcoholic
wishes to buy some rope.

It can be flax,
or better yet hemp,
reasonable price preferred.

He is of black and briny bent,
long trained in the art of knotting
in methodical despair, all alone
he tars his boat, mends the sails.

Water gushes from heaven's gates.

§

Three in the cave:
man, woman and sword.
All else is just shadow play.

Did I mention fire?
Fire was and is
forever future, kingdom come
in cave, in crypt, in script.

A primal rite binds words –
rhythm magic,
hum and hymn in sync
after the world –

for the world.

§

When the fear of death looms large
so that all flight is futile,
we make haste to greet it.

We hurl ourselves into the abyss,
head for the gas oven
or through the mirror.
Any which way.

Fear is the gravest
gravitation.

§

Grey matter and dark matter
wrestle in silence.
                    And now –
a glint darts swiftly
off Occam's razor!

No need for haste, Hamlet.

There is only one road
that is sure –
like the swirl of a snail shell
or the flight and fall of down.

§

You are no better than anyone.
You are no worse than anyone.
You have been given the world.
Look what there is to see.

Nurture what is around you,
nurture who is beside you.
All creatures in their own way
are funny.

All are fragile.

§

On behalf of all
who have been lost at sea,
on behalf of all
who have lost hold of the day,
I pray this day
in the shrinking light of tapers
from a tired heart's last
pain and passion.

Come,
tramps, crooks, cripples,
vagabonds and courtesans,
pimps and palmists,
loafers, liars, junkies,
scabs, spendthrifts, boozers;
you who are frightened, famished, frozen,
who are born fatherless,
whom the world has shunned,
who are lost and long distraught –
you shall rest in the softest beds
this night.

For you I spread a table,
fine wines and choice dishes –
come, come.
I know you well,
your blood might be mingled in mine...

Only for one does the gate fall silent.
Only you I do not know,
sadist.

§

I sing in praise of the loser
for the winner is well lauded,
I kneel before the forlorn,
I bow before the beaten.
The world-quitter creates,
discovers selfdom in dreams;
the reality-bearer holds
strength and stature untold.

I sing in praise of the loser
and for the have-not's joy;
I crown the outcast, pressing
my lips to that noble brow –
to the one who labours
lifelong with lack and loss,
both lightly and upright,
I am true to the core.

§

When no matter how you ask,
your roots find no earthly vigour,
when your wrists are ripped raw
by the brutal chain of wrongness –
turn to the steep cliff face,
press there your fair lips
and speak water, pure water.

§

Nothing else have I asked, nor will I –
a clear heart is my only request –
the will to mirror the sky
in response to the refracting world.

Give me moments of light in blood,
in spirit, so that I may find my way:
give my soul grace to bestow mercy,
give me fortitude to remain fair.

§

All you need will come your way
in one or another veiled form.
If you recognise it,
it will be yours.

All you want will come your way,
it will know you inside and out.
Breathe, count to ten.

The cost comes later.

§

Nothing is happening. Just stars circling
and worlds forming, falling, flickering by the second.
Their tremulous dust, light-laden on my eyelids,
I sense like a far-off whiff of childhood, when I simply knew:
                                        yes, it will happen.
(God...God!)

Nothing is happening.

From hair root to foot sole –
a lightning strike pierces and you spin, speechless,
in cosmic solitude, in eternal inquiry
amid hollowness and wholeness, boundless being.

Whisper-sighs, shrill cries, snippets of rambling
you seem to hear in the oddly distant din of the universe –
shadows, shimmies, traces of things fancied, things faced –
though nothing is happening.
                                Even your inmost
magic molten fire, fluid trickling word magma
refuses to harden into a song-like line.

Nothing is happening.
Just stars circling;
the heart, saline and crystalline, throbs alone, ticks true.

World, let me off.
World, yes: I'm through.

Nothing is happening,
just stars circling
in cosmic solitude, in eternal inquiry
amid hollowness and wholeness, boundless being…

§

To live more clearly,
I plumb the depths
of language and dream,
hoping to hit upon
a vision unveiled.

Whoever, whatever the case,
the rule of the game is the same:
to catch – so as to
let go.

§

My load I now give away.
Take it and bear it, earth,
as my mother once bore me.

My wishing I now give away.
Take it and whirl it, wind,
as my father once whirled me.

My fear I now give away.
Who wants it may take it;
I do not fear any more.

Clouds' Letter to the Sand

§

Observing the rainbowing world,
                    I opted for black
as my emblem of life; motherblind pre-
lude of love, prescience of pulsing truth
deep in preter-worlds, right here
behind the eyes.

All things run their course, collapse,
                            come back,
present another face – I know it well,
I know by heart that granite hand,
                        that ample lap.

Amid the glittering riot of colour,
the surging blaze, stands a figure tall and black,
                            bound for the void.
The bundle at his feet suddenly forms
an exclamation dot.

§

Go on then, sun,
take my spring-shy body,
which has frozen with time –
ever since you crossed
the tropic and were lost.

There is nothing new here –
winter wolves and summer gnats –
and a drowned sailor's bride
who mindlessly wanders
the watery rim of the world.

§

A house by the sea
forever feels like a ship
just put ashore.

Every night it roams
across endless oceans,
ages and spaces.

All around is a drift of stars,
deep within weeps a hearth
that no one will light.

As a dog misses its master,
so the house by the sea
pines for its captain.

§

All that is is utterable
in another language
we forget at birth.

The odd word still comes to mind –
as we stroll by the sea perhaps
without a thought, without a care,
without a single cent...

The stones speak it slowly –
not a hint of an accent.

§

Stark and scant is the nordic light.
Sledges are heavy shadow drawn,
owls and wolves keep watch.
The Word grinds between teeth.

I don't even know how to be here.
I freeze in the grip of history.
All borders are binding,
each story is sealed.

What I'm talking about is
the dustmote dance
in the fathomless sun.

§

Tomorrow is the light of all.

Folding the world up as well as out
flipping the pages, reading the stars,
losing the thought
that was the source.

It runs rings in the blood
and is still to be written on water.

§

I lingered long by the sea
idly combing the beach
for this and for that.

Back home I tipped out my bag:
eleven stones and a single
birdshitty poem.

§

The vivid display of life flows on –
no fits and starts, no flights of fancy,
free and infinitely faceted,
still and full of force.

The art lies in deciding
where on earth art begins.
The counter of waves may lose
sight of the ocean.

§

Clouds' letter to the sand:
    shade fades away.

On our other side
    day holds sway.

§

Who lives in light never wanes.
Who belongs to the universe
is allotted to all,
is never spent.

Like a stone that lets itself
be polished by waves.
Like a looking glass
on which the sun shines:

light that casts no shadow,
fire that does not burn.

§

The scalpel and the metronome
on my father's piano
kept silence between them
when I was a child.

Only now, given time,
have I started to hear
and to heed
their strange tales.

They trim time to a sliver.

§

Chant the mantra, mandragora,
mandragora, deathly deep sleep-weed:
it all keeps turning, keeps churning,
keeps occurring.

Enduring is the evidence
that of all forces the most intense,
the most immense
is love's essence.

§

Love treads a quicksilver path,
yet its spirit seems to lie dreaming
in almost all that you touch.

Softly skywards unfurls the seedling,
its face in the sway of the sun.

Of all instincts this feels
the deepest.

§

You ceased to be a miracle
for me. I figured
you out.

And yet
that gleam of clarity,
that ethereal glow
does not desert you.

How does it feel to be you?

How does it feel to be a flower,
a tree, the sky?
How does it feel to be a thought?

§

To make a human life visible
and give it to many
for ever
will fail.

A distance remains,
a tinge of estrangement.

Only deep wisdom, immense love
gathers and binds
our distinctions.

This spirit
of light and liberty,
which awakes at once
in two bodies

aware of itself
in both.

§

Bird spell opens the bashful bloom of day.

A rapturous, rampant surge,
a sigh
from bosom of earth to spreading branches
a tinkling of leaves like tiny bells.

Luscious and light is the waking
of fragrant thought, trickling bliss,
richly resounding echo of longing
like a church bell across water.

§

With a feather in the sand, a flowering branch in the air,
a finger on your naked back
I write the secret word –
                    primordial, tender and mighty,
untamed by thought, unfettered by language.

A drop of light dangles in the water,
a dazzling flash, snapshot and revelation:
                    wind as old as the world
on its way by way of us.

§

I am your land.
   Tough, beyond storms. Your boat wrecked
on the rocks. The sea cast you onto my coast
when you had surrendered all hope, sure
in yourself that you shared a familiar fate.
Whoever hit dream shores was reeled into
roving, whoever took heart, would lose...
Chaos, maelstrom, foam.
   You caught your breath on my beach, on my breast.
Then raised your head and pledged. You stared –
rosehip, shingle and stone. No cedars, no
palms. But
   still I am your land. Vision and vastness,
your blue land – mist-streams, night-dreams,
a crisp mirage of sea foam and cliffs,
of grief and peace. Land that has led to
legends, so far a source only of salt,
a little bread and fresh water, frequent
falling stars...
   Land – wild, lofty, luminous, where
the very stones sigh in bliss – where,
thinking of you, the rivers run pure milk and
honey...

§

Days dissolve like sugar lumps
in the coffee night.

Oh how delectable,
mmm, more and more tempting.

OM, entranced tremors from
the domed drum of the world.

§

No will to do aught.
Only murmur. Through the body
the universe unfurls, effulgent,
eloquent.

Arousing aroma of thought,
an ancient urn yields to the touch.
No desire dismissed out of hand,
no surprise deemed out of reach.

§

The gentlest in you is sheltered in me,
the strongest in you surrounds me.
We are one and the same body
where soul and spirit dance free.

We rest from the weariness of the world,
and the anguish of insecurity –
greeting each morning as the first,
meeting each evening as the last.

§

You open me up like a tome treasured
by a bibliophile,
you read, riffle and read,
and I feel such pleasure and pride.

You know me by heart –
so you simply savour
oh so slowly, one at a time
my tendermost words.

If this isn't poetry,
I don't know what is.

§

And I love you
because I love you.

Why even meet –
you are mere air to me.

There everywhere.

§

And the bells tolled; July's glory
played itself out. Your mouth
roamed over my body
like a lamb astray –
here nibbling at desert grass,
there uttering plaintive baas,
then pausing as if scenting danger.

I'm afraid, we will not meet again.

As I said, we will no longer seek
the enchanted vaults of the night.
Those bridges are burned.
As I said, I'm afraid: those tender,
living lips like wounds
will still touch me in memory;
will stay and stalk me.

And the bells will toll on and on.

§

If autumn is endured
to the very end, then comes spring,
I believe.

Trees that now watch over
our sadness, open once more
for the miracle of light.

Beneath the broad leaves
is where we will meet,
my love.

THE VISITOR

The door barely creaked,
opened by the wind perhaps.
All were seated at the table,
silently eating dinner.

When I raised my eyes,
I saw you in the doorway.
You stood there smirking –
as only you do.

I set down my cup and stood up.
It was all I could do.
You looked at me long
and your glance was sad.

Strange,
you had hardly changed at all.
Just your mouth bore a deeper
line of bitterness.

I wanted to invite you in,
but all of a sudden
the walls began to sway
and broke into a spin.

I closed my eyes.
When I looked, the door was shut.
All were just as before,
silently eating dinner.

§

No other or better world will come
for us. Nor can a single deed
be altered.

Wind and sky are not the same
as yesterday.
No, not a single foothold beyond
our fragile borders.

Only light.

§

In the house I was passing a phone rang.
No one responded.

But I recognised the voice of my long-gone
love.
How else could he reach me
here, in this strange city,
how else could he touch me
with his unforgettable hand?

Fountain spray misted
my bare-skinned shoulder,
through empty streets there flittered
a sad smile – a butterfly.

I dwelt in two worlds at once,
in between times,
alone at heart.

Death counted days
while love prayed.

§

Wherever I set foot, you
are my axis. Your spirit,
Silent One, enfolds me.

No, I won't flee. Nor fall,
treading unsteady heights.
No, I won't drown. Your trust
holds me secure in your thought.

In you, I am ensconced,
you, my inmost pain,
you, my impossible beauty,
you, my longing.

§

What is not and yet is
all the time alluding.
Hear all who may.

I believe in life and self,
all-pervading spirit,
silence beyond words.

§

Life will become eternity
after one has gone.

In the trees, in the breeze
I can hear His call.

I feel the torrid breath of fire,
the dark beat of blood.

Life will become eternity,
once these doors have gone.

§

A ship with hoisted sails
draws near my shore.
I sense it, I feel it
and stand in a cold sweat.

A ship with holy sails
that flies no flag –
oh, how I have waited
childlike in wastes of death.

Day declines and darkens.
Dead of night.
Will it come – will it not?

All passes so imperceptibly.
All arrives
on the quiet.

§

Light, light is the ship that ferries
through dream lagoons
all your thought and despair
that find no place in world;
glance-light and stalwart it glides
in full sail beneath the Milky Way,
between towering bare cliffs
through the foam of breakers;
round headlands, through inlets,
through enchanted lagoons
and flowering reefs of coral.
Light, light is the ship that quickens
image and desire in your blood;
your thought and despair
and radiant power and peace.

Leeward into the Light

§

I dreamt about the world.
                    Out of its mind,
it sought to surround me, to overlap
the shores of my imagination.
No,
I whispered; no, I seek something else –
I seek the unexpected,
infinite as the universe –
                    a new
invigorating molten essence.

World, oh world, be more!
I begged.

Thus it was born;
        the answer I asked for
shattered me;
        the light blinded me,
a blast from the bedrock of the world
severed my hopes layer by layer,
and scorching, it altered me
        beyond recognition.

Godforsaken, trembling and naked,
I woke –
        to a rain of stars.

In shy desire I stretched out my hand.
And I laughed out loud,
        grasping the dream

I had about the world –
a dream about love;
a dream.

§

I had a dream that Satan spoke
in your voice. In the midst of slow
rack and ruin, he gave me a bowl
of blown glass and said: 'Behold.
                    Here is death.'

§

Shadow-like you move among the shades,
softly jangles your dark chain.

Countless are the foundlings that gather
around the glare of the fire.

You walk away, you walk on by,
melting into darkness as if into water.

You stand on the bridge on your own.

Spectral mist swirls round the trees.
Softly jangles your dark chain.

§

I slept the sleep of minerals,
I slept like magma
and I had a vision: a shimmering wind
rose menacing beyond the mountains.

Days all melted to a single tear,
a song of praise rose from my throat,
a lively, scintillating fire crystal
aswim in my shifting shape.

§

The world as pleasure and pain?
The world as thought.

A broken electric cable in your warm palm,
naked writhing lightning: decide!
Shadow over your hands.

A ring's secret ciphers conceal message
and mode.

You spell out pain and mercy
and light spills from your eyes.

The pattern of the world shoots
forth the snake that bites its tail.

Amid essences, extracts, eccentric
riddle of the self, there appears

on your forehead a trillion-image
incandescent crystal –

that does not pale.

§

Stay uncut crystal.

Don't consent to be honed
into a crown jewel.

Let no war be waged
because of you.

§

Two.
There are two whom I ask,
to whom I give ear,
whose judgement I fear.

The pendulum swings through silence,
sand trickles through empty space –
ever nearer. Every instant.

I waver wanly between the two
half blindfolded,
now this way
now that way
inclining, declining.

Less and less is the leeway between them,
straighter and straighter is my spine,
shorter and shorter steps,
on and on
rarer and rarer the air –

until in the deep mirror of dream
they meet and meld
in a single gleam –
my heart and death.

Ash into air.

§

Through the mist-dark park
dreams are still lured
to a creaking stair and hook
that took our wings without a word.

The moment stalled, swelled
and soared –
the startling speed of sincerity.

All eras converge at once.

Revealed in a streak of light
above our bed, the swell
of the mirror ceiling.

§

Life and dream – leaves
from the same murmurous tree
and voluminous book.

Who reads in reams lives,
who leafs at leisure dreams.

Life and dream – two sisters.
The third, most taciturn, is death.

§

I went to visit the world.

How it smelt,
how it moved and hummed!
The blood stirred in my arm – svelte,
vein-blue and sluggish –
the blood stirred and a deluge of darkness
stained all the luminous rooms!

I am alone again now.
My sadness
is angular, guarded and grim.

§

The world slips the mind, mutates and melts.
All that collects, clusters, recoils.
Roaming in the blood is star salt,
pounding in memory a purple pulse:
do not believe it! Your being has been.
Do not worry – it recurs in the head.
What truly never has been
is only and always at hand.

§

Now it has come; what you call autumn.
The air fills with glass temples, silent tremolo.
A black stork stands in my room.
A fan fetches elsewhere, breath wends in and out.
Evenings pass unnoticed. I scarcely stir from my book.
There is no honey so pure that tastes like you,
nor thoughts so pure.

Script collects on my brow,
the mark of a sword.

Tranquil, clear and golden, imposing voice of dreams.
I sense it, unseeing.
Though I am seen through
by autumn.

From empty glass temples
the black stork takes to the air.
Wing beats, leaves of an open book, flutter of a fan,
living breath, low tremolo.
There is no honey so pure, no thoughts so pure as you.
You know this world lasts no more than an instant
of infinite peace.

§

All seems so clear in September –
yet for all the stars that fall,
not one lands in your palm.

Instead they reflect in headwaters
just like crystals of salt
or tears shed by God.

If you put your hands together,
your palms between them will cup
the taste of the dawn of the world.

§

The husk of home houses two worlds,
two hemispheres, halves of the brain,
time in frames.
                Only blood on its rounds
holds them together – in ever-quivering flight,
enchantment and tremor and tension.

§

Rain, are you still rain
when you do not fall?
Dream, are you a dream
when no one sees you?

Whose are these steps
on this bare and mute
mist-buried mountain?
muses the listener.

The walker's mind wanders.
Through the listener's dream
seeps a drizzle of steps
like Yggdrasil leaves.

§

Snow is a blank sheet.
                Underneath
ciphers glow unseen –
the trumpet solo of spring,
the saffron shade of summer.

Snow is a blank sheet.
                Do not write
there a single name;
let stars be reflected
in countless crystals.

Each flake is a star,
altogether unique
in insignificance –
                all dissolves.

Snow is a blank sheet
and solace –
                silence of language,
aquiver with meaning.

§

Dauntless, defenceless
the word of truth
dazzles in the light of dawn
like a mountain lake,
like deepest desire –
limpid, vivid and lucid.

Surreal and clear
is its diamond colour.

§

Do not fear, do not worry
or strike a pose.
Who you meet in each mirror
comes and goes.

Your body is a cocoon. Slumbering within
sways the soul of the world.

When it wakes it spreads its wings,
in a sudden swoop
all the stars draw near:
tintinnabuli!

The ring of infinity
straight and scintillating.
The mind stirs from the lustre of silence.

§

She never thinks about money,
for her father is very high up.
Alone, the child of God,
dances down roads like the wind.

In a storm or in a steeple,
on a bridge over falling water
softly and surely she sways
like a sufi or as if in a swoon.

§

Some words are precious as stones
found from the ground or the mind,
whether all on their own
or in the secret talk of the dead.

What could be more momentous,
more unique or more profound?
Some words are softer than air
and harder than any diamond.

§

If you long for the sea,
be a river.

If you like, I'll tell river truth:
that road does not run uphill.

The river road skirts the hill.

§

I watch my hand in the flowing water.
It does not sink, it does not float.
The light quivers.
My mind is neither tense nor tranquil.
The riverbed shows – though not the depth.
The palm of my hand does not show.
The water is calm and cool.
Algae all adrift,
a few yellow leaves glide by.
I watch my hand in the flowing water.
It follows the watcher.

§

Whatever you get
your hand does not grip.
You never wonder
what will stay or slip.

Whatever you take
is there to be shared –
the song-wave within
casts shells ashore.

Spray wets your cheek
in the storm that seethes,
you stand like an onlooker
strangely at ease.

Surely you feel
for that throb an affinity,
as there opens within you
a door to infinity.

§

Stepping out of the church porch
leeward into the light,
do you notice the lilac?

A treasure trove lies below,
tucked away from troubled times
beyond the waves of war.

Shielded by silver words
is the gold of silence.

That will definitely get you
a ferry ticket
to infinity.

Write when you arrive.

§

Between the dead and the living
is a wall of cliff,
within it glints
the spirit stone – spectrolite.

Sometimes at night I carve
upon it letters and prayers,
mirrorwise they may be read
by some who have left our sight.

§

A stairway, a sky snail-shell,
unwinds step by step, year by year,
its wake fading.

Only weariness grows and bestows
heavy, red and rampant blooms,
sometimes even fruit.

A rain of spores and sparks.
Words
gush from eyes and ears.
Breath.
Silence.

Breath,
the blinding glare of emptiness.

The sky snail-shell unwinds
into lingering luminance,
into original formlessness.

One more step
then the mind within will see
the mind without.

LESSON IN HARMONY

As a child of four or five, I used to long for paints and paper so that I could draw to my heart's content. My father gave me a piece of plain cardboard, a glass of water and a fine paintbrush, and said: this is all we need. To prove his words, he took the wet brush and sketched a landscape on the cardboard. By the time he reached the bottom corner, the top of the picture had already started to fade. For me, this magical boundless landscape remains a symbol of human existence. Our means are limited, our possibilities limitless.

At Tallinn Academy of Music where my father used to work, his official title was Master of Harmony. This never ceased to amaze me, for he was a choleric individual, a chain smoker and an alcoholic whose whole life was in opposition to the *sectio aurea*, the balance point of the pendulum which he as an admirer of Greek culture so ardently championed. Only later did I understand that perhaps the essence of harmony is embodied in striving, not in surviving, in never-ending movement, in resetting the balance moment by moment. Or perhaps survival becomes possible only through striving – like riding waves on a surfboard.

Isn't what we call beauty in fact essentially grace? Grace – so different in a tiger or a gazelle – is born through perceiving oneself and the surrounding world clearly, through correctly evaluating one's possibilities and using them to the full. Grace can only increase by way of precision, unlike strength, which can increase endlessly. Grace is strength with intelligence, the skill of making do with little, the capacity to recognise what is necessary, and the courage to give up what is superfluous. Grace is born from trust, which takes many forms. A child trusts naturally, as long as he has not experienced disappointment. A pilot, on the other hand, trusts because of experience and being in control. A lover trusts – believes, hopes, loves – in spite of everything and risking all. Love blinds fear, just as fear may blind love; they exclude one another. The trust of a lover – opening up in all one's vulnerability – is the greatest expression of humanity. It gives rise to supreme grace – the perception of one's place in the world, one's fragility and fortuity – and a readiness to act nonetheless, that ultimate devotion and creativity.

My first book of selected poetry in 1991 was called *Days of Grace* (*Armuaeg*); this is a legal term denoting the time between the pronouncement of capital punishment and its implementation. The whole of human life may be interpreted as days of grace – being aware of one's mortality but not of the moment of death. Born out of love, we are at the same time born for love; that time – the length of which we cannot know, though we can intuit its depth – gives us a chance to realise love, to do good, to at least strive towards what we consider most important and valuable at any given moment.

Towards the end of his life when my father lost both his legs and the ability to move his right hand, he rebuilt his piano with his remaining left hand. At night, tortured by phantom pains that did not let him sleep, he created what may be the best opuses of his life. By day, he took endless pictures of the view from the window of the small apartment in which he lived. For my father, even the tiniest change – a pram hoisted onto the balcony of the house opposite, a passing bird, a shower of rain – was worth recording. Only years later did it occur to me how these numerous, repetitive packs of photographs in their own way rhymed with the piece of cardboard from my childhood. When there is no more space, time expands.

At my father's deathbed, I held his hand, feeling his soul leave his body. His last words, uttered with half closed eyes, were: 'Up… up…' And then, still guessing, I understood: when there is no more time, space expands.

Doris Kareva is one of Estonia's leading poets. She was born in Tallinn in 1958, daughter of the composer Hillar Kareva, and published her first poems at the age of 14. In 1977 she entered the University of Tartu as an already acknowledged young poet. Due to her dissident connections she was expelled but graduated as a distance student in Romance and Germanic philology. She has worked for the cultural weekly *Sirp* (Sickle) and as the Secretary-General of the Estonian National Commission for UNESCO from 1992 to 2008, and is currently an editor for the literary journal *Looming* (Creation).

Following the restoration of Estonian independence, Kareva's collection *In Place of the World* received the national cultural prize in 1993. She used the prize money to set up the 'Straw Stipend' for the publication of debut collections, to support emerging talent in unsettled times. Kareva has published 15 collections of poetry, a collection of essays and a work of prose. She has also translated poetry (Anna Akhmatova, Emily Brontë, Emily Dickinson, Kabir, Rumi) and plays, essays and prose (W.H. Auden, Samuel Beckett, Joseph Brodsky, Kahlil Gibran, Shakespeare). She has compiled anthologies, written texts for music and theatre, and given lectures on culture, education and ethics in Estonia and abroad. Her poetry has been translated into over 20 languages and has inspired composers and directors in Estonia and abroad – sounding equally fitting at a punk concert and the funeral ceremony of a president, in a Warner Classics studio and at the Estonian Song Festival. Kareva has been honoured with two national cultural prizes and four literary prizes; in 2001 she was awarded the Estonian Order of the White Star.

She has two books of poetry in English translation, *Shape of Time*, translated by Tiina Aleman (Arc Publications, 2010), and *Days of Grace: Selected Poems*, translated by Miriam McIlfatrick-Ksenofontov (Bloodaxe Books, 2018).

Miriam McIlfatrick-Ksenofontov is a lecturer and freelance literary translator from Northern Ireland who has lived in Estonia since 1991. Her scholarly interests include comparative poetry, cognitive poetics, the oral poetic tradition and the poetics of translation. She translates Estonian poetry primarily for performance at festivals and collaborates with musicians, poets and artists. Her translations also regularly appear in journals and anthologies; recent publications include *Six Estonian Poets* (with others, Arc Publications, 2015), Kätlin Kaldmaa's *One is None* (A Midsummer Night's Press, 2014), *Contemporary Estonian Poetry, A Baltic Anthology: Book Three* (with others, University of New Orleans Press, 2013), *New European Poets* (with others, Graywolf Press, 2008) and *Black Ceiling: animated poetry* (with others, Eesti Joonisfilm, 2007). Her translation of Doris Kareva's *Days of Grace: Selected Poems* was published by Bloodaxe in 2018.

Together with Doris Kareva she co-edited the bilingual Estonian-English anthology *Windship with Oars of Light* (Huma, 2001) and *Rogha Dánta: seven Irish women poets in Estonian* (verb, 2005). In 2015 she was guest-editor and co-translator of 'Writing From the Edge: Estonian Literature', an Estonian special issue of *Words without Borders*. Her own poetry has appeared in Estonian translation by Doris Kareva and she was awarded 2015 annual prize for poetry by the Estonian literary journal *Looming*.

.

www.ingramcontent.com/pod-product-compliance
Lightning Source LLC
Jackson TN
JSHW011940131224
75386JS00041B/1480